THE DARKEST DAY

A Liturgy and Dramatic
Monologue for Good Friday

WILLIAM GRIMBOL

C.S.S. Publishing Company, Inc.
Lima, Ohio

THE DARKEST DAY
A Liturgy and Dramatic Monolog for Good Friday

Reprinted March 1989

6807 / ISBN 0-89536-789-0   PRINTED IN U.S.A.

Part 1. The Order of Service

A Liturgy for Good Friday

SILENT MEDITATION

SILENT PROCESSION *(Pastor and choir enter darkened sanctuary)*

THE OPENING HYMN "Were You There When They Crucified My Lord?"

THE CONFESSION

> **Leader:** *We come here together in a spirit of full humility and complete honesty.*
>
> **People:** *We come here knowing that we share in Judas' betrayal, for we have so often chosen to turn our backs on Christ.*
>
> **Leader:** *There are so many simple ways that we reject and repudiate Jesus Christ . . .*
>
> **People:** *Our greed . . . our selfishness . . . our apathy . . . our indifference . . . our bigotry . . . our bloated pride . . . our possession by possessions . . . our addiction to achievement and accumulation . . . our insane idolatries of pleasure and youth . . . our cynical hopelessness . . . our fear of being persons of conviction and courage . . . our lack of faith in times of crisis, are all ways that we simply say no to Jesus Christ.*
>
> **Leader:** *Let us not, then, blame Judas as the source of all shame, as the symbol of all betrayal.*
>
> **People:** *Like Judas, we too are human, and we too are guilty of massive betrayal. Like Judas, we too are in need of greater faith, and the gift of your embrace of grace.*
>
> **Leader:** *Like Judas, we too seek your forgiveness.*

THE ABSOLUTION

THE SCRIPTURE Matthew 27:3-9, 15-26, 35-40, 45-54

THE ANTHEM

THE HYMN OF THE DAY "O Sacred Head, Now Wounded"

THE MESSAGE "The Ghost of Judas" *(A Dramatic Monolog)*

THE CREED

THE OFFERING

THE OFFERTORY

THE LITANY

> *Leader:*   *Lord, heal us of our need to betray you.*
>
> *People:*   *Free us to become your people, a people dedicated to discipleship, and committed to the spirit of the cross.*
>
> *Leader:*   *Free us to know that we are forgiven, and that it is our status as forgiven sinners that empowers us to transform the world.*
>
> *People:*   *The world can indeed become your kingdom . . . a kingdom of peace and justice and equality . . . a kingdom blossoming with hope, and bursting forth with joy . . . a kingdom not of power and pride and possessions, but of service and sacrifice and suffering in your name.*
>
> *Leader:*   *Into your hands . . .*
>
> *People:*   *We commend our spirits.*
>
> *All:*   *We let go, we let God. We become his children. We become his slaves, and, in so doing, we become, for the first time, fully free. Amen*

THE CLOSING HYMN "In the Cross of Christ I Glory"

THE BENEDICTION

SILENT MEDITATION

SILENT RECESSION *(Pastor[s] and people depart quietly)*

Part 2. "The Ghost of Judas"

A Dramatic Monolog

The Ghost of Judas

(Judas enters in darkness, attired appropriately in black biblical-looking garb. The lights should come up slowly as he begins to speak.)

I'm sure you have already guessed who I am.
It's Good Friday, and I'm your perennial scapegoat . . . you know
. . . the Betrayer . . . that is my label, as if I had invented
the word, or inspired its creation.

Good Friday, and now all of you can blame me, you can blame
me for sending him to the cross.
Me, Judas Iscariot, the ultimate traitor, the villain, I'm responsi-
ble, aren't I?
Judas Iscariot, why I've outdone them all, every last traitor in the
books . . . Benedict Arnold and Lady Macbeth couldn't hold
a candle to me . . . I personify the word TRAITOR.

So it's Good Friday again, is it?
You gather here together solemnly — and then you feign anger
and disgust at me in your liturgies, and then you hurl insults
at me and blame me for it all, but . . . BUT . . . do you ever
learn anything, do you ever learn anything about YOUR-
SELVES on Good Friday . . . do you . . . do you LEARN anything from this experience?

Well, *[today/tonight]* I'm here to see to it that you do.
[Today/tonight] I, the Ghost of Judas Iscariot, will make sure you
understand just how much alike you and I are.
I want you to know that I am no misfit — no oddball — no nut
— no raving lunatic.
NO, I am a human being, or at least I *was* — one who made a
mistake; a *big* mistake, yes, but a mistake *you* make too.
Yes, you do.
I want to be sure that on this Good Friday you come to know who
I really am, and what my relationship to Christ was all about.
I, the Ghost of Judas, want you to know the man — the person
— the human being — that you have labeled as THE ULTI-
MATE BETRAYER.

[Today/tonight], you will have learned something other than blaming me; [today/tonight] you will learn to relate to me, relate so closely I think the sweat will start to pour from the heat of our intimacy, the hell of our common bond of sin.

Let me get started.

"Why did he pick me?" you ask.
I know you roll that over and over again in your mind on this day.
"Why Judas?" Why?
Because I believed.
I believed in him.
I found in him the answers to all the questions that ever infested my soul.
I found his smile to be an embrace that took away my fear, that answered the riddle of just why I was here.
His eyes — oh, his eyes could instill in me such a longing to love others, to love him, that I felt as if I would burst at the seams of my heart.
I *believed* in him.
He picked me because I believed.
He picked me because I followed.
I followed, and I went through it with him.
I followed through all the insults, all the persecution, all the nights of tension, wondering if we'd see the sunrise.
I followed him even when I wondered down deep, "Is he really . . . is he the One?"
When down deep inside me there was a nausea of doubt that wanted to heave up my insides in every direction.
I followed because I saw in him all that I ever wanted to be, all that I believed I *could* be, all that I felt life was to reveal about the worth and value of life.
You can take a lot away from me — my name, my respect, my reputation — but you can't deny the reality that I followed, that I picked up my cross, that I risked it all, and followed — you can't deny me that!

Christ knew that. He knew I believed. He knew how much I wanted to be his disciple.
I *know* he knew.

Let me ask you a question:
Would *you* have followed?
Would *you* have joined that band of twelve?
Would *you* have suffered the hunger, the thirst, the fear, the
   humiliation, *the doubt?*
Would you have followed him for even a day?
Can you answer that honestly?

Jesus knew.
He knew that inside me I had a pool of tears that only he could
   swim across; he knew that I wanted to understand the move-
   ment of the stars and the rise of the sun; he knew that I needed
   to be needed so badly it hurt; he knew that he alone could
   give my life a sense of purpose and hope again.
He knew.

He knew what it was like to be alive in those times — times when
   nobody knew when the next war would hit, or the next famine,
   or the next earthquake; times when you could see the violence
   in your neighbor's eye; times when you trusted nobody: not
   the government, nor your religious leaders, nor your friends;
   not *anybody;* times that held no hope, no promise, no expec-
   tation of anything other than getting worse.
He knew.

He knew that he alone was the answer — the Living Truth.
Yes, he was the Living Truth, an answer to the gaping jaws of
   humanity which screamed "Why?" every day and every night.
He was that one and only answer.
He knew I believed.
He also knew that I would fail . . .

I'm sure of it — I know he was aware that I had a tragic flaw —
   a tragic flaw that would cost both of us our lives.

My flaw!
My terrible flaw!
This is where you people make me the angriest.
"*My*" flaw.
Mine?

It is *our* flaw.
It is the *human* flaw.
Money.
That is the flaw: money.
And it isn't my sole possession, the curse of greed; the curse of
   believing in money as our salvation is not mine alone.
He knew it was my flaw.
I know it is mine.
Is it yours?
Is it?

How many times have you betrayed Christ for a buck?
How many times have you betrayed your Christian ethics so you
   could get ahead, or be more successful, or fit in at the Club,
   or so you could be admired by your competitors?
How many times?
How many times have you betrayed Christ by making his minis-
   try your last budget priority?

So I sold him for thirty pieces of silver — in your language, twenty
   bucks.
So I compromised my integrity for twenty miserable bucks.
So I sacrificed my soul for money.
So is *that* so new?
Is that so different?
NO, it is so common it stinks.
Why do you think sixteen of the thirty-eight parables were about
   money and our stewardship? Why?
Because when Christ taught (and I counted and listened to all six-
   teen repeated over and over again, and I still didn't hear) —
   when he taught, he was vividly conscious of our human flaw:
   THE IDOLATRY OF MONEY; THE IDOLATRY OF POS-
   SESSIONS AND POWER.

Judas Iscariot, the betrayer, the human being who betrayed Christ
   for a buck.
My flaw, my tragic flaw, the lust for money, a lust for thirty silver
   coins *I didn't even need, I didn't even want,* but *somehow* I
   just had to have.
Am I so different from any of you?

Can you explain why you need so much you know you don't need?
Can you explain your luxurious so-called necessities?

The other disciples rejected me and scorned me, and they too spit
    on the life I had lived; they too blamed me and used me as
    the scapegoat; they too tried to explain my actions without
    looking inside themselves.
They denied him.
They doubted him.
They fought over more status and reputation with him.
They slept while he suffered.
They got drunk when he needed them.
They too had the flaw; it was just that I was the one who fulfilled
    the prophecy.
They said I was always money hungry, that *that* was why I was
    their treasurer, and that I even stole from that leather purse.
That was a lie!
I was treasurer because I was the only one who was not from
    Galilee; I was the odd man out, and so they gave me the dirty
    job of treasurer.
I did *not* steal that money!
Any one of them could have done it!
That is the real issue: they *all* had their eyes on it at one time
    or another.
Anyone — any human being — could have taken it.
I refuse to be the BAD DISCIPLE, while they are all elevated like
    mini-Gods.
Like all the others, I was chosen.
I believed.
I followed.
I was not an "evil man."
I was not a BAD DISCIPLE.
They were not perfect either.
They were not SAINTS.
They too sinned, all of them.
I cannot be blamed for all the evil ever committed against Christ.
It is not fair.
It is not right.

Don't get me wrong.

I'm not saying I'm innocent.

No, I claim my guilt.

I have spent an eternity grieving over my actions.

But you must keep it in perspective, or at least learn from my mistake.

I claim my sin, but I will not claim all of *your* sin, nor all of the sin that brought Christ to the cross.

You know something?

There is one lesson from my story that I'm sure you missed; one lesson that is the most essential of all; one lesson that is, in fact, the message of Christ to everyone every day.

That lesson is this: my sin — my horrible sin — WAS FORGIVABLE.

Christ would have forgiven me.

I know that now, I know that he would have.

I committed suicide.

I took my life because I could not cope with my grief, I could not accept my guilt, I could not tolerate the terribleness of what I had done.

I hated myself so much that I wanted to see every ounce of evil breath come out of me.

I was in despair, and that was my real unforgivable sin, not because Christ refuses to forgive it, but because it despairs of the possibility of being forgiven.

Christ died for me, too.

He died for my sins as well.

Never forget the reality of his love.

Never forget that he refuses to give up on you, even when you have.

Never forget that he wants you to love life, he wants you to live a life of love.

My unforgivable sin.

Not the betrayal.

Not the suicide.

No, it was the refusal to be forgiven.

In that, too, I am like you.

In that, too, I share your humanity.
In that, too, I am one with you.

I, the Ghost of Judas, am here to tell you that you are forgiven
— you are loved — you are chosen — you have value and
worth — so follow — follow him who is still my Lord.
Follow him who, I know now, was my Savior.

Follow.
Please learn that *[today/tonight]*.
I beg of you . . . follow . . .
(Judas leaves.)

(Blackout)

www.ingramcontent.com/pod-product-compliance
Lightning Source LLC
Chambersburg PA
CBHW060046040426
42331CB00032B/2501